CW00401073

Body, Re
(Cavafy Poems)

Ian Parks

Calder Valley
Poetry

Published 2018 by Calder Valley Poetry
www.caldervalleypoetry.com
caldervalleypoetry@yahoo.com

ISBN 978-1-9997062-2-1

Designed and typeset in Garamond by Bob Horne

Printed by Amadeus Press, Ezra House, West 26 Business Park,
Cleckheaton, West Yorkshire, BD19 4TQ.
www.amadeuspress.co.uk

*Acknowledgements are due to: Lampeter Review, Modern Poetry in
Translation, and Strix.*

A number of poems were written during a residency at Gladstone's Library.

Contents

Constantine Cavafy died in Alexandria in 1933. Shortly before his death at the age of seventy he took Holy Communion at the Orthodox Church. His last act was to trace a circle on a piece of paper and then place a full stop at its centre. It was a suitably enigmatic end to a life spent in exile in Alexandria where he wrote his poems almost in secret, shunning publication and sharing them only with a select circle of friends. His reputation as one of the finest Greek poets of the twentieth century followed only after his death.

This collection is a companion to *If Possible* which was published by Calder Valley Poetry in 2018. I first came to Cavafy's poetry through W. H. Auden who admired him and drew attention to his 'unique tone of voice'. Before publishing an article of mine on Cavafy's poems, the editor of *New Walk Magazine*, Rory Waterman, suggested that we include a poem by him. He went on to suggest that I might provide the version. That poem was *Candles*, the first of Cavafy's poems that I attempted. Without that suggestion this collection would never have happened. There are several good translations of Cavafy available. I wanted to avoid a literal word-for-word rendering, preferring instead to try and capture something of the atmosphere and tone of this remarkable poet. I had no intention, either, of attempting anything comprehensive. Cavafy left behind around one-hundred-and-fifty poems but I only wrote the poems I was drawn to; the ones I had some empathy with as a poet. My hope is that they convey something of the flavour of the originals.

for Mick Jenkinson

Body, Remember

Body, remember how much love you drew –
not just the beds, the hot illicit rooms
but how that love so fiercely burned
deep in the eyes of those that gazed on you:
how voices trembled even though
some random moment always intervened
to stop the dream from coming true.
Now everything is contained in the past
it feels as if, in fact, you gave in to
all those desires that fiercely burned;
remember, through the eyes of those that gazed on you,
or the voices trembling. Body, remember.

The Bandaged Shoulder

He told me that he'd had a fall
but I suspected something else –
another reason for the secret wound
on his white shoulder that the bandage hid.

As he was overreaching to take down
a book of photographs
the bandage loosened and came free.
He didn't flinch. I took my time
and bound it tenderly.

Because it came from love, from him
the fresh blood stirred me inexplicably.
After he'd gone I found beside his chair
the coiled, unravelled dressings on the floor.

Instead of throwing them away
I took one of the sullied linen strips
and pressed it to my mouth –
the blood of love imprinted on my lips.

The Ides of March

Be careful soul, be on your guard
against ambition, fame and glory –
or if you must pursue them do so cautiously.
Be hesitant before you act
and if your actions take you to the heights
you'll need to be more searching than before.

When you become like Caesar, when you reach
the point at which you're unassailable, secure –
a person of authority and power,
trailing in your wake a scraping retinue –
be vigilant when you walk down the street.

Take notice when a stranger hurries up
breathless from the milling crowd,
pressing an urgent letter in your hand
and saying *Read this, Caesar, before you go,*
there's something here that you must see.
Make sure you pause, make sure you think again
before you speak; turn down whoever bows
and supplicates. The Senators can wait.
Don't put it off, discover straight away
the warning in that letter meant for you.

Prayer

The mother of a sailor drowned at sea
is praying where the votive candles burn.
She kneels before the Virgin, asking her
to bring her boy back peacefully to shore,
to let the trade winds blow him safely home.
The icon hears: unblinking, powerless
but distant; solemn, gracious, sad.
She knows what the mother cannot know –
that the son she prays for never will return.

Before Time Changed Them

It caused them so much grief
to say goodbye as circumstance
not choice forced them apart.
One left to make a living on another continent;
the other stayed behind. The truth is
love was already fading when he went,
its first heat cooling irrecoverably.
Perhaps fate intervened
to come between them then –
an author altering the plot
before time changed them into what they are,
one seeming to the other to remain
forever a young man of twenty-four.

Exiles

Alexandria persists. To walk
the length of this long road
that ends outside the Hippodrome
is to see the ancient city at its best.
Despite the ravaged temples
and the residue of war,
despite neglected gardens
and the shrunken populace,
the city still survives.
Time passes pleasantly for us
in private study and in walks.
At night we go down to the shore –
a group of Greeks disguised
by different names – and talk about
the latest news from Rome,
discuss affairs of church and state.
Of course we keep opinions to ourselves.
Last night we read some poetry:
an epic which we all pronounced was fine.
All of this is bearable because
we know our exile won't last long.
On that we're all agreed.
The word we hear is positive.
A few more months of this
and then our allies will prevail.
We'll overrun the rulers here
and then it will be us who will decide
just who to forgive and not forgive.

Long Ago

There's something I want to recall –
something thinned and faded by the years
because it happened long ago.

I want to give the memory a voice,
something immediate and precise.
A jasmine skin, a summer night.
Eyes of blue … a sapphire blue … blue ice.

White Flowers

They used to sit together there
inside the café where his friend had said
It's no use. We can't afford
to be together anymore.
I'm tired of these cheap cafés, cheap hotels,
the empty pockets, empty days.
Besides, I've been approached by someone else.
He's promised me two suits, silk handkerchiefs.

And so to win his lover back
he did whatever he had to do
and scraped together just enough.
His friend came back for twenty pounds.
Not just for that, he told himself,
but for the intimacy between them,
the closeness that they'd shared.
That someone else turned out to be
a liar and a cheat – a someone else
who went back on the promises he made:
one suit instead of two
and that after much pleading by his friend.

Three months on he doesn't need
the suits or handkerchiefs,
not twenty pounds or even twenty pence.

Sunday last they laid him in his grave
at ten o'clock, a week ago today.
He placed white flowers on the coffin lid,
the loveliest white flowers that became
someone of his rare beauty and his youth.

After they'd put his friend in the ground,
chance took him to the café where they met.
The place itself seemed dead.
He looked into the emptiness and felt
a corkscrew turning in his heart.

Envoys

The gifts they brought to Delphi were magnificent.
They astounded everyone. For centuries
all the treasure they'd received
was nothing in comparison to this –
the untold riches sent by them,
two Ptolemaic brothers, rival kings.
But now they have them firmly in their grasp
the priests grow anxious and distressed.
Their combined years of skill, experience
will be required of them as they decide
which brother to let down and disappoint.
Secretly, they meet by candlelight
to weigh their options carefully.
Before they're done the envoys hurry back.
The oracle won't be approached at all,
no consultation on the merits of
the brothers or the offerings they made.
They pack their bags and leave at once for home.
It comes as a relief to all the priests
who get to keep the treasures anyway
without the risk of causing great offence.
But why this sudden change of heart, this haste?
The priests don't know that only yesterday
the envoys had received some startling news:
the oracle had been pronounced in Rome.

The Mirror

There was a mirror in the wealthy house.
Tarnished, hung there eighty years ago,
it took up half the hall.

From the tailor's where he worked
a young man sauntered in with a new suit
and waited patiently for the receipt.
In the few moments when he was alone
he smoothed his hair, straightened his tie,
then took the receipt and walked away.

Grown used to people, objects,
all the things that came and went
across its face for all those years
the mirror was enlivened by
the vision it had seen,
held onto his reflection
long after he had gone.

Poseidonians

After centuries of mingling their Greek blood
with foreigners in a foreign land
they lost the language that they used to speak.
Of all the fine traditions handed down
from their great ancestors
one festival remained, full of garlands
and religious rites, sweet music, races, sacrifice.
And as the hectic days drew to a close
they wondered what those ancestors had meant
reviving all the ancient names in Greek –
a Greek that no one seemed to understand.
Because of this the festival seemed sad.
It had a far-off, melancholy air:
no celebration but a pained reminder of
the fact they'd once been true citizens of Greece
but fallen and debased, so isolated
and removed from the pure Hellenic life.

Julian at the Mysteries

In the deep cavern hid from light
among a band of pagan Greeks
the disembodied forms appeared to him,
their haloes shining in the dark.
Julian panicked, crossed himself

by habit almost, as he used to do
and instantly the vision disappeared.
The Greeks exchanged a knowing glance.
Apprehensively, young Julian said
It's true I'm frightened and I want to go

but none among you can deny
the miracle you saw; the way
the demons scurried out of sight
the moment that I made the cross.
But they'd have none of that.

To think you'd try to hoodwink us they laughed.
Go ply your tricks with bishops and their priests
but not with us. The gods of Greece appeared to you
in all their glory and you looked the other way.
They were offended by your gesture

and only left because you made
that crude, disgraceful sign.
So Julian believed them and he went
convinced by the unholy arguments
of sophists and philosophers.

Morning Sea

I stop and look. The morning sea is blue,
made bluer by the cloudless sky.
The beach is radiant in the yellow light.
I want to take in what is there

in all of its simplicity – the morning sea,
the cloudless sky, the stretch of yellow shore –
pure, direct, uncomplicated by
my dreams and recollections:
those sensual thoughts I see things through.

Ammonis

They want you to produce an epitaph
for Ammonis the poet now he's gone.
If anyone can do him justice it is you.
Something measured, Raphael, and refined.

You'll obviously praise his poems –
those things of beauty that contain
the beauty that resided in his soul.
You'll need all the skill that you possess

to pour Egyptian feeling into your Greek lines.
Try too to infuse them with a sense
of our lives also, how we live them here.
We want you to aspire to greatness now

to pen a fitting tribute to our brother
so that the rhythm running through it makes it clear
this is a paean from the heart
of one Alexandrian to another.

The Picture

I'm absorbed by my work –
absorbed and diligent. Today
I find it's going very slow.
The day itself has pulled me down
into its dark pit. All this wind and rain.
I'd rather look than speak.
My inclination draws me to
the picture that I'm holding now –
a young man resting by a spring
worn out, I'd say, from running there.
Refreshed from drinking at the stream
he sleeps under a perfect sky.
Recovering my art through art
I sit and gaze at it for a long time.

Aristovoulos

King Herod hides his face and wails.
His grief can't be contained:
it reaches out from him to everyone.
Grief for Aristovoulos who drowned.
That harmless bit of horseplay in the pool.

When word spreads into Syria
the poets and the sculptors will be sad.
They'll mourn a beauty that they never saw
but heard about, imagined, made their own.
But nothing they imagined could compare
with the native grace and beauty of this boy.
No god whose statue stands in Antioch
can rival this true son of Israel.

His sister Miriam, Herod's wife, cries out.
All Alexandria joins her in her grief.
Behind closed doors she changes tune,
curses her faithless husband for his lie.
How did that old fox fool her?
How did he manoeuvre to destroy
the last of the Asmoneans,
the last of that great line?
She hates herself for failing to protect
or notice even what was being done;
how Kypros and Salome – those two whores –
had finally prevailed,
whispering their poison into Herod's ear
and helping him to hatch his scheming plot.
They're laughing at her now behind her back.

Worst of all she must pretend
that she believes their lies,
grieving outward as she hates inside.
She's powerless to go out and proclaim,
to tell the waiting Jews
who was responsible for that sad death,
how the murder was committed
and the truth of how that prince of Israel died.

Chandelier

In the centre of that small
and empty room – a room
encased entirely in green –
a crystal chandelier,
its points of light

engendering a fever that still burns.
The radiance of that hot fire
consumes. Not for the cautious
or discreet the yearnings they illuminate,
the passions they ignite.

Dimitrios

Dimitrios had a perfect grasp
of what it means to be a king.
When the Macedonians wanted someone else
to rule instead of him
he took off his golden crown
and let his purple robe fall to the floor.
Like an actor who has played his part
he left those props behind.
Changed into a simple rustic gown
he slipped unnoticed, out through the side door.

Resurfacing

One o'clock perhaps or half past one.
A hidden recess in the public bar
partitioned off and out of sight.
You and I and emptiness,
the waiter dozing near the door
under a green lamp leaking light.
Our shirts unbuttoned in the summer heat.
July was burning up outside,
our clothes abandoned, half undressed –
your hands all over me.
All I need now to recollect
that rare intensity
are the images that still survive
the sad demise of what we used to be.

Waiting for the Barbarians

The barbarians are almost at the gates.

Why are we waiting in the crowded marketplace?
Why doesn't the senate make new laws?
There's no point making any laws at all.

The barbarians are almost at the gates.

When they arrive laws will be obsolete.
They'll be the ones who legislate.

Why is the emperor up before the dawn
enthroned in purple, wearing his golden crown,
preparing to submit and supplicate?

Because the barbarians are due today
and their leaders will be offered a fine scroll
with honorific titles and great names.

Why are our councillors making such a show,
parading through the forum in their rich embroidered
        gowns?
They've brought out their rings of emeralds, their shining
        amethysts.
The barbarians are dazzled by such things.

Why don't our politicians make their speeches?
Because the barbarians bore easily;
they don't have the time to listen to such rhetoric.

Why is the city centre emptying?
Why are we abandoning the public thoroughfares?
And why has such confusion spread?
Each citizen is making his way home
absorbed in thoughts they don't want to express.

Because the night has fallen and another day has passed
and the rumour starts to spread
that the barbarians aren't at the city gates.
They've crossed the border swiftly and are gone.

What will we do without that constant threat?
The barbarians were a solution after all.

The Wine Bowl

This order I'm working on now,
commissioned by a rich and noble house –
a patron with the most exquisite taste –
features my trademark waterfalls and vines.
Made of the purest silver it outshines
the finest of the work I've done before.
The figure that I placed below the rim,
the centre of the flowers and the streams,
is naked, one toe dipping in, an object of desire.
I needed to invoke the gods of memory
to help me with the task of forming him
so that the youthful face I'd loved
was a true likeness of that matchless boy.
But even that was not enough.
You'll know why when I tell you how he died
fifteen years ago, a soldier on the battlefield.

Half an Hour

I never had you and I know
I never will. At best a word or two
like last night in the crowded bar –
a smile, a glance, a brief exchange.
There's a sadness to it I confess.
Yet those of us who give our life to art
can sometimes make a moment so intense
it feels as if we've lived it in the flesh.
Helped by the bottle, I indulged.
I think you knew the game I played
and likewise played your part,
lingering on deliberately.
Neither imagination nor the alcohol we shared
could compensate for lips and eyes,
the closeness of your hand to mine.
Half an hour was not enough.

The End of Antony

After he'd fallen on his sword
he heard the women wailing –
the Queen of Egypt and her train
lamenting in their less than perfect Greek.
The excesses of his Alexandrian life
repelled him now. He longed for home.
The foreign culture he'd embraced
seemed shallow, empty, sickening.
His Latin blood surged through him
and he said *Stop crying for me.*
Your lament should be a eulogy
for all the great things that I've done:
I was a soldier and a hero among men
and if I die, I die without disgrace.
There is no shame in how I met my end:
a son of Rome defeated only by a son of Rome.

Grey Opal

Looking at this opal makes me think
of those grey eyes that once I loved:
eyes I looked into deeply for a month
before he took a job and moved away.

Where did he go to? I forget.
It must be all of twenty years and yet
it seems like yesterday. Eyes of opal. Opal eyes.
Those eyes have lost their lustre
and that lovely face has aged –

but, memory, if you can bring them back
bring back a memory of that love.
Make it come alive again tonight.

Kaisarion

My intention was to check the facts,
to pass a quiet hour or two
among the names and faces of the past.
The volume that I chose contained
a history of the Ptolemies.
The praise becomes monotonous:
the men are just, magnificent and bold,
the women upright, beautiful.

Just as I was about to close the book
and place it on the shelf
I came across the briefest mention of
Kaisarion – Little Caesar, Caesar's son.
I was drawn to it inexplicably.

You stood there full of poise and charm.
Because the record is so sparse
I filled the sketch out in my mind;
made you sensitive and shy –
a dreaming, far-off face
despite the name they gave you, King of Kings.

So vivid did I conjure you
that as the lamplight dimmed
you came into my darkened room,
came close and stood in front of me
wearing the expression that you wore
in fallen Alexandria,
imploring them to pity you –
Octavian's henchmen, those murderers
who said *One Caesar is enough.*

Locked from Sight

He dresses the shop window carefully,
arranges all his wares so they can catch the light.
When customers come in to buy
he brings out trays of bracelets, pendants, rings –
precious objects meant to impress.
But ruby roses, lilies of pearl, and violet amethysts
made from love, from pure disinterestedness,
his inner vision burning bright,
he wraps up lovingly in green silk
and places in a safe. Those items aren't for sale.
When someone comes in from the street
he interests them in what's on show.
His exquisite work, the things he values most
are kept under the counter locked from sight.

Longings

Like bodies of the beautiful who died before their time
wept over in a silent sepulchre
with roses at the head and jasmine at the feet
so are the longings that went unfulfilled, that never once
felt the burning touch of passion in the night
or woke to dawn's bright radiance.